תְּפִלַּת שַׁחֲרִית לְשַׁבָּת

THE SHABBAT MORNING SERVICE

BOOK 2

The
Shabbat Amidah

עֲמִידָה לְשַׁבָּת

תְּפִלַּת שַׁחֲרִית לְשַׁבָּת

THE SHABBAT MORNING SERVICE

2 The Shabbat Amidah

עֲמִידָה לְשַׁבָּת

Commentary by Jules Harlow

Exercises by Roberta Osser Baum

BEHRMAN HOUSE

Designer Robert J. O'Dell

Illustrator Nachman Levine

Project Editor Ruby G. Strauss

ISBN: 0-87441-432-6

Manufactured in the United States of America

INTRODUCTION

This is the second book in a series of three. In the first book you learned to read and understand the Shema and its Blessings (קְרִיאַת שְׁמַע וּבִרְכוֹתֶיהָ). In this book you will study the Amidah (עֲמִידָה).

The Hebrew word עֲמִידָה means "standing." We stand when we recite the Amidah. The Amidah is known by other names as well. It is called the "Silent Prayer" because it is said quietly, in a very soft voice. It is also called the "Shmoneh Esreh" (the Hebrew word for eighteen). The weekday version of the Amidah originally contained eighteen blessings. It continues to be called the "Shmoneh Esreh" even though the version now recited on weekdays consists of nineteen blessings and even though the version we recite on Shabbat and the holidays consists of only seven blessings. The ancient Rabbis called the עֲמִידָה the prayer, showing its special importance in Jewish tradition.

Every service contains a version of the Amidah. Regardless of the occasion, the first three blessings and the last three blessings are always the same. Only the middle section changes. On weekdays, the middle section of the עֲמִידָה consists of thirteen blessings. On Shabbat these thirteen are replaced by one blessing expressing the special qualities of the day.

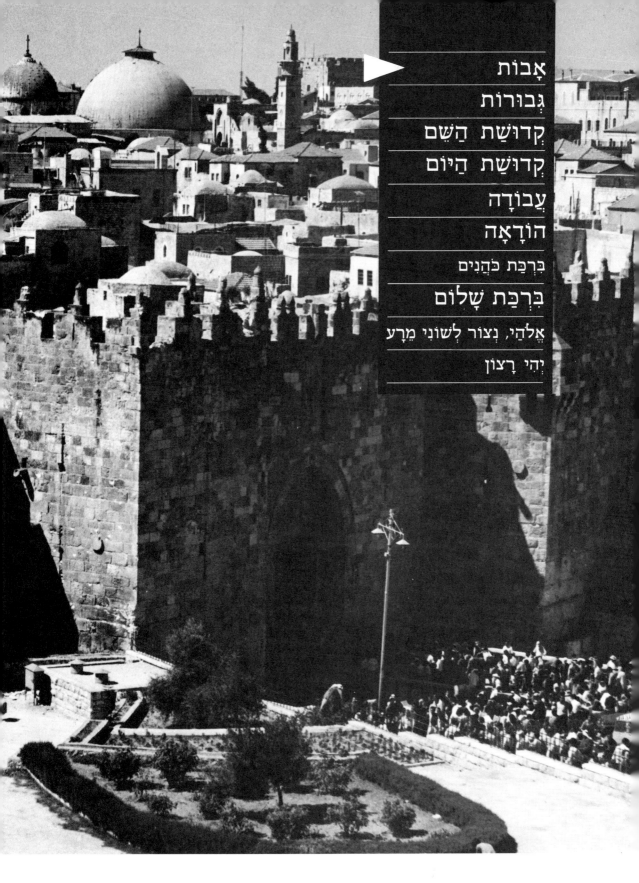

The first three blessings of every עֲמִידָה are the same. The first בְּרָכָה praises God and His relationship to the Jewish people since the beginning of our history. The blessing is called אָבוֹת *(fathers)* because it addresses God as the "God of our fathers," the patriarchs Abraham, Isaac and Jacob. We praise God as we recall our ancestors' love for Him. Because of their good deeds and His love, God will bring a redeemer to their children's children after them.

אָבוֹת

Before we begin the עֲמִידָה, we recite this sentence:

1 אֲדֹנָי, שְׂפָתַי תִּפְתָּח וּפִי יַגִּיד תְּהִלָּתֶךָ

Lord, open my lips and my mouth will declare your praise.

2 בָּרוּךְ אַתָּה יְיָ אֱלֹהֵינוּ וֵאלֹהֵי אֲבוֹתֵינוּ, אֱלֹהֵי

3 אַבְרָהָם אֱלֹהֵי יִצְחָק וֵאלֹהֵי יַעֲקֹב, הָאֵל הַגָּדוֹל

4 הַגִּבּוֹר וְהַנּוֹרָא, אֵל עֶלְיוֹן, גּוֹמֵל חֲסָדִים טוֹבִים

וְקוֹנֵה הַכֹּל, וְזוֹכֵר חַסְדֵי אָבוֹת וּמֵבִיא גוֹאֵל 5

לִבְנֵי בְנֵיהֶם לְמַעַן שְׁמוֹ בְּאַהֲבָה. מֶלֶךְ עוֹזֵר 6

וּמוֹשִׁיעַ וּמָגֵן. 7

בָּרוּךְ אַתָּה יְיָ, מָגֵן אַבְרָהָם. 8

Blessed are You, O Lord, Shield of Abraham.

The first blessing of the עֲמִידָה is called _____.

אָבוֹת means _fathers_____.

Read the introduction. Find another English word for "fathers":

_____

Our fathers were _Jacob___, _Isac___, and _Abraham___.

Their Hebrew names are: אַבְרָהָם יִצְחָק יַעֲקֹב

Find and lightly underline the names in the prayer passage.

Write the name that is read in the concluding sentence of אָבוֹת:

_____

אָבוֹת is a בְּרָכָה.

The phrase בָּרוּךְ אַתָּה יְיָ appears in every בְּרָכָה.

Find and lightly underline this phrase in the last sentence.

Complete the final sentence in אָבוֹת.

בָּרוּךְ_____

This sentence has been translated for you.

Copy the English meaning here: _____

_____

What do you think this sentence means?

_____

_____

אֱלֹהֵי
God of

אָבוֹת
fathers

אֲבוֹתֵינוּ
our fathers

יַעֲקֹב
Jacob

יִצְחָק
Isaac

אַבְרָהָם
Abraham

לִבְנֵי בְנֵיהֶם
to their children's
children

חַסְדֵי
kind deeds

וְזוֹכֵר
and remembers

חֲסָדִים טוֹבִים
loving kindness

וּמָגֵן
and Shield

וּמוֹשִׁיעַ
and Redeemer

עוֹזֵר
Helper

מֶלֶךְ
King

גּוֹאֵל
Redeemer

עֶלְיוֹן
supreme

וְהַנּוֹרָא
and the revered

הַגִּבּוֹר
the mighty

הַגָּדוֹל
the great

Choose the correct KEY WORD. Write it next to the English translation.

God _____ our Fathers _____

Abraham _____ Isaac _____

King _____ Helper _____

Savior _____ Shield _____

Read the KEY WORDS to fill in the correct answers.

אָב means "father".

Write the Hebrew for these 2 words.

_אֲבוֹת_ _____

Fathers   our fathers

Circle אב in each word.

אב is found within the name of one of our forefathers.

Write his name here: _(אַבְ)רָהָם_

Circle the word אב in his name.

His name means "father of a mighty nation".

אֲבוֹתֵינוּ means _Our fathers_

Write the Hebrew names of our fathers

Yacove   _Yitsach_   _Avraham_

Jacob   Isaac   Abraham.

Read this phrase: אֱלֹהֵינוּ וֵאלֹהֵי אֲבוֹתֵינוּ

"our God and God of our fathers"

Write the Hebrew phrase: _____

Find and lightly underline the phrase in the בְּרָכָה.

We ask God to remember His relationship with our fathers.

The Hebrew word for and remembers is _וְזוֹכֵר_

אָבוֹת speaks of four roles God plays in the lives of His people.

Write the Hebrew for each of them.

_____ _____ _____ _____

Shield   Redeemer   Helper   King

These four words are used in אָבוֹת to describe God.

_____ _____ _____ _____

supreme   and the revered   the mighty   the great

READING CHALLENGE

Can you read line 1 without a mistake?

Can you read lines 2 and 3 without a mistake?

Can you translate these two lines?

You have learned all the words.

_____

_____

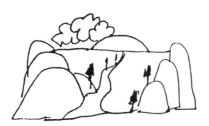

God's name is written in different ways:

אֱלֹהֵי   אֱלֹהִים   אֵל   יְהוָֹה   יְיָ

Write the three forms of אֵל found above:

_____

Read line 2 in אָבוֹת.

Write the three words derived from אֵל:

_____

Write: the word meaning "our God": _____

the two words that appear again in line 3:

_____

a third form of אֵל read in line 3: _____

Write the two forms of God's name pronounced the same way:

_____

Say these two words.

Sometimes this pronunciation is written out.

It looks like this: אֲדֹנָי

Write it here. _____

Find אֲדֹנָי in line 1. Lightly circle it.

Write the three forms of God's name that are pronounced exactly the

same: _____

ROOTS

Hebrew verbs and nouns are constructed from groups of letters called roots. Each root has a meaning that can be found in a Hebrew dictionary. A root almost always has three letters. A root has no vowels. Many Hebrew words can come from one root.

ח־ס־ד is an important root.

ח־ס־ד means "kindness" or "goodness".

Write the three root letters: ___ ___ ___

The root ח־ס־ד is found in lines 4 and 5.

Find and lightly underline the two words.

Write the two words. Circle the root letters in each word.

_____   _____

Read your KEY WORDS. Write the Hebrew phrase for "loving kindness" as it is found in אָבוֹת:

_____

READING CHALLENGE

Can you read lines 2-5 in אָבוֹת without a mistake?

Fill in the missing words.

_____ _____ _____ וּפִי יַגִּיד _____

_____ _____ _____ _____ בָּרוּךְ אַתָּה יְיָ אֱלֹהֵינוּ, _____

אַבְרָהָם _____ יִצְחָק _____ יַעֲקֹב, הָאֵל _____

_____ _____ _____ _____, אֵל _____, גּוֹמֵל

_____ _____ וְקוֹנֵה הַכֹּל, וְזוֹכֵר _____

_____ _____ _____ וּמֵבִיא גוֹאֵל לְמַעַן שְׁמוֹ

בָּרוּךְ _____. _____ _____ _____ מֶלֶךְ _____

_____ _____ _____. אַתָּה

Can you read the entire בְּרָכָה without a mistake?

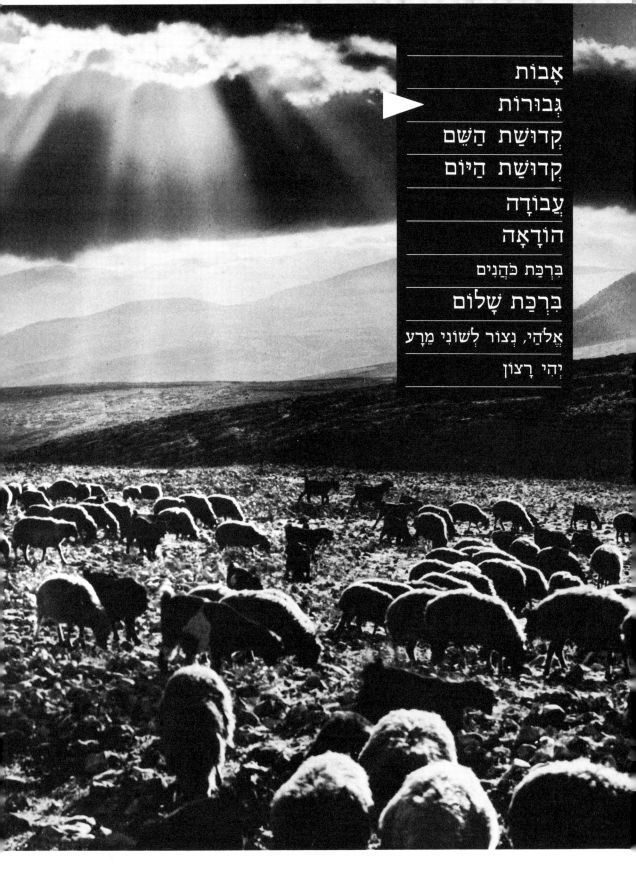

The second blessing of the עֲמִידָה is called
גְּבוּרוֹת. גְּבוּרוֹת means *powers*. The בְּרָכָה
celebrates God's power in nature and in our lives.
It speaks of God's power to give life to the dead.

גְּבוּרוֹת

1 אַתָּה גִבּוֹר לְעוֹלָם יְיָ, מְחַיֶּה מֵתִים אַתָּה, רַב
2 לְהוֹשִׁיעַ.

From Shemini Azeret until Passover add:

3 מַשִּׁיב הָרוּחַ וּמוֹרִיד הַגָּשֶׁם.

You cause the wind to blow and the rain to fall.

4 מְכַלְכֵּל חַיִּים בְּחֶסֶד, מְחַיֶּה מֵתִים בְּרַחֲמִים
5 רַבִּים, סוֹמֵךְ נוֹפְלִים וְרוֹפֵא חוֹלִים וּמַתִּיר
6 אֲסוּרִים, וּמְקַיֵּם אֱמוּנָתוֹ לִישֵׁנֵי עָפָר. מִי כָמְוֹךָ
7 בַּעַל גְּבוּרוֹת וּמִי דְוֹמֶה לָּךְ, מֶלֶךְ מֵמִית וּמְחַיֶּה
8 וּמַצְמִיחַ יְשׁוּעָה. וְנֶאֱמָן אַתָּה לְהַחֲיוֹת מֵתִים.
9 בָּרוּךְ אַתָּה יְיָ, מְחַיֵּה הַמֵּתִים.

Blessed are You, O Lord who gives life to the dead.

The second blessing of the עֲמִידָה is called _____.

גְּבוּרוֹת means _____.

Find and lightly underline this word in line 7.

Complete the phrase (beginning in line 6):

מִי כָמוֹךָ _____ _____ וּמִי _____ לָךְ

"Who is like You, Almighty God, and who can be compared to You?"

Read these words that describe God's powers:

סוֹמֵךְ נוֹפְלִים וְרוֹפֵא חוֹלִים וּמַתִּיר אֲסוּרִים
וּמְקַיֵּם אֱמוּנָתוֹ לִישֵׁנֵי עָפָר

"You uphold the falling, and heal the sick, and set free those in

bondage and keep faith with those who sleep in the dust"

Fill in the missing Hebrew words:

סוֹמֵךְ _____ _____ וְרוֹפֵא _____ וּמַתִּיר _____

וּמְקַיֵּם _____ לִישֵׁנֵי _____

Find and lightly underline these ten words in the passage.

The last line of גְּבוּרוֹת contains the three words found in every

בְּרָכָה.

Complete the בְּרָכָה.

בָּרוּךְ _____

KEY PHRASES TO READ AND UNDERSTAND

אַתָּה גִבּוֹר לְעוֹלָם יְיָ

You are mighty forever, O Lord

מְחַיֵּה מֵתִים אַתָּה

You call the dead to
everlasting life

מְכַלְכֵּל חַיִּים בְּחֶסֶד

sustain the living with
loving kindness

בְּרַחֲמִים רַבִּים

in great mercy

סוֹמֵךְ נוֹפְלִים

uphold the falling

וְרוֹפֵא חוֹלִים

and heal the sick

וּמַתִּיר אֲסוּרִים

and set free those in bondage

וּמְקַיֵּם אֱמוּנָתוֹ לִישֵׁנֵי עָפָר

and keep faith with those who
sleep in the dust

Write the Hebrew for each phrase:

You are mighty forever, O Lord

_____

sustain the living with loving kindness

_____

in great mercy _____

uphold the falling _____

and heal the sick _____

and set free those in bondage _____

Read the KEY PHRASES. Fill in the correct answers.

The phrase that introduces גְּבוּרוֹת:

_____

Turn back to page 14.

ח־ס־ד means _____ or _____.

Write the phrase that contains the root ח־ס־ד: (page 19)

_____

מְחַיֵּה מֵתִים is read three times in גְּבוּרוֹת.

Write the two words: _____ _____

Find מְחַיֵּה מֵתִים each time it is read and lightly underline it.

Read the sentences that contain the phrase מְחַיֵּה מֵתִים.

ר־ח־ם means "mercy", "compassion", or "pity".

Write the KEY PHRASE that contains the root ר־ח־ם:

_____

These four phrases refer to God's powers.

Write them in the correct order.

וּמַתִּיר אֲסוּרִים ־ וְרוֹפֵא חוֹלִים ־ וּמְקַיֵּם אֱמוּנָתוֹ
לִישֵׁנֵי עָפָר ־ סוֹמֵךְ נוֹפְלִים

_____

_____

The word אַתָּה is often used when speaking to God.

אַתָּה means "You".

Write the Hebrew. _____

How many times does the word אַתָּה appear in גְּבוּרוֹת? _____

Lightly circle it each time you find it.

Can you read each sentence that contains the word אַתָּה without a mistake?

אַתָּה appears twice in one of the sentences.

Read that sentence once again.

READING CHALLENGE

Can you read the entire בְּרָכָה without a mistake?

Can you read גְּבוּרוֹת אָבוֹת and without a mistake?

21

גְּבוּרוֹת

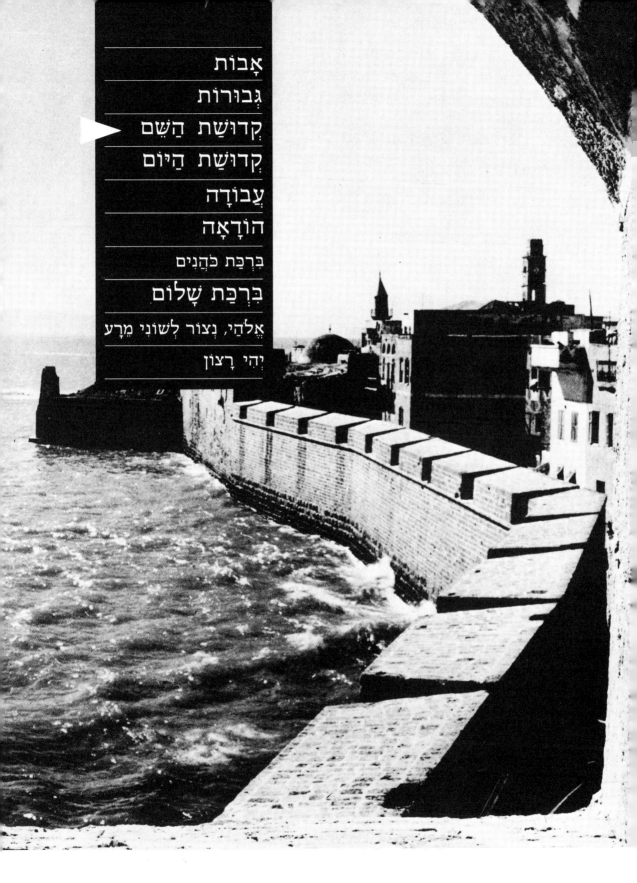

The third blessing of the עֲמִידָה is קְדֻשַּת הַשֵׁם, the Holiness of God (literally, the holiness of *the* name). Since קְדֻשַּת הַשֵׁם praises God's holiness, the word קָדוֹש (*holy*) appears often in the blessing. When the עֲמִידָה is repeated aloud by the leader of the service, another version of this blessing is recited. That version is called קְדֻשָּה.

קְדֻשַּת הַשֵׁם

When the עֲמִידָה is recited silently, only the following three lines are recited. They are omitted by the leader when the עֲמִידָה is recited aloud.

1 אַתָּה קָדוֹש וְשִׁמְךָ קָדוֹש, וּקְדוֹשִׁים בְּכָל-יוֹם

2 יְהַלְלוּךָ סֶּלָה.

3 בָּרוּךְ אַתָּה יְיָ, הָאֵל הַקָּדוֹש.

The leader recites the עֲמִידָה aloud only if ten adults are present (a מִנְיָן). When the leader recites the עֲמִידָה the third blessing differs from the one recited by individuals. The קְדֻשָּה follows. The indented lines are recited aloud by the Congregation.

4 נְקַדֵּשׁ אֶת-שִׁמְךָ בָּעוֹלָם, כְּשֵׁם שֶׁמַּקְדִּישִׁים אֹתוֹ

5 בִּשְׁמֵי מָרוֹם, כַּכָּתוּב עַל יַד נְבִיאֶךָ, וְקָרָא זֶה

6 אֶל זֶה וְאָמַר:

We celebrate God's holiness on earth, as the angels celebrate it on high, with words from the vision of the prophet Isaiah:

7 קָדוֹשׁ קָדוֹשׁ קָדוֹשׁ יְיָ צְבָאוֹת,

8 מְלֹא כָל־הָאָרֶץ כְּבוֹדוֹ.

Holy, holy, holy, Lord of hosts; the whole world is filled with His glory.

9 אָז בְּקוֹל רַעַשׁ גָּדוֹל אַדִּיר וְחָזָק מַשְׁמִיעִים

10 קוֹל, מִתְנַשְּׂאִים לְעֻמַּת שְׂרָפִים, לְעֻמָּתָם בָּרוּךְ

11 יֹאמֵרוּ:

12 בָּרוּךְ כְּבוֹד יְיָ מִמְּקוֹמוֹ.

13 מִמְּקוֹמְךָ מַלְכֵּנוּ תוֹפִיעַ וְתִמְלֹךְ עָלֵינוּ, כִּי

14 מְחַכִּים אֲנַחְנוּ לָךְ. מָתַי תִּמְלֹךְ בְּצִיּוֹן, בְּקָרוֹב

15 בְּיָמֵינוּ לְעוֹלָם וָעֶד תִּשְׁכֹּן. תִּתְגַּדַּל וְתִתְקַדַּשׁ

16 בְּתוֹךְ יְרוּשָׁלַיִם עִירְךָ, לְדוֹר וָדוֹר וּלְנֵצַח

17 נְצָחִים. וְעֵינֵינוּ תִרְאֶינָה מַלְכוּתֶךָ, כַּדָּבָר

18 הָאָמוּר בְּשִׁירֵי עֻזֶּךָ, עַל יְדֵי דָוִד מְשִׁיחַ צִדְקֶךָ.

19 יִמְלֹךְ יְיָ לְעוֹלָם, אֱלֹהַיִךְ צִיּוֹן לְדוֹר וָדוֹר,

20 הַלְלוּיָהּ.

The Lord will rule forever. Your God, O Zion, for all generations. Praise the Lord.

21 לְדוֹר וָדוֹר נַגִּיד גָּדְלֶךָ, וּלְנֵצַח נְצָחִים קְדֻשָּׁתְךָ

22 נַקְדִּישׁ. וְשִׁבְחֲךָ אֱלֹהֵינוּ מִפִּינוּ לֹא יָמוּשׁ

23 לְעוֹלָם וָעֶד, כִּי אֵל מֶלֶךְ גָּדוֹל וְקָדוֹשׁ אָתָּה.

24 בָּרוּךְ אַתָּה יְיָ, הָאֵל הַקָּדוֹשׁ.

The holiness of God is the theme of קְדוּשַׁת הַשֵׁם and the

קְדוּשָׁה.

The root ק־ד־שׁ means "holy".

Write the root here: שׁ ד — ק

The theme of God's holiness is repeated many times in the בְּרָכָה.

Write each word built on the root ק־ד־שׁ.

line 1   ק־ד־שׁ

line 7   ק־ד־שׁ

line 4   וְקִדּוֹשִׁים

line 15   וְתִתְקַדֵּשׁ

line 21   קְדֻשַּׁת

line 22   בְּקִדְשֵׁי

line 23   לְקָדוֹשׁ

line 24   הַקָּדוֹשׁ

Read lines 7 and 8.

Fill in the missing words.

וִי־   צְבָאוֹת   מְלֹא   כָּל־הָאָרֶץ

    כְּבוֹדוֹ   מְלֹא,

"Holy, holy, holy, the Lord of hosts. The whole world is filled with His glory."

קְדוּשַׁת הַשֵׁם

קְדוּשַׁת הַשֵׁם concludes with the words found at the end of every בְּרָכָה.

Complete each בְּרָכָה.

בָּרוּךְ _____

Write the English meaning here: _____

_____

READING CHALLENGE

Can you read the words built on the root ק־ד־שׁ in

קְדוּשַׁת הַשֵׁם without a mistake?

Can you read the sentence beginning קָדוֹשׁ קָדוֹשׁ קָדוֹשׁ

without a mistake?

Can you read the concluding sentence of the בְּרָכָה without a

mistake?

A SUFFIX IS A UNIT OF MEANING ATTACHED
TO THE END OF A WORD

The suffix ךְ means "Thy", "You", "Your".

Add the vowels to complete these words:

שמך	נביאך	ממקומך	עירך	מלכותך
line 1	line 5	line 13	line 16	line 17

עזך	צדקך	אלהיך	גדלך	קדשתך	ושבחך
line 18	line 18	line 19	line 21	line 21	line 22

Can you read each word you completed without a mistake?

AN IMPORTANT ROOT

ה-ל-ל is an important root found in many prayers.

ה-ל-ל means "praise".

Write the root: ____ ____ ____

Write the word in line 20 built on the root ה-ל-ל: _____

קְדוּשַׁת הַשֵׁם

There are three congregational responses in the בְּרָכָה.

The responses are indented.

Write the line number for each response: first _7-8_, second _12_,

third _19-20_

These three responses are written below in mixed-up order.

Write each response correctly.

מָלֹא יְיָ קָדוֹשׁ צְבָאוֹת כָּל־הָאָרֶץ קָדוֹשׁ
כְּבוֹדוֹ קָדוֹשׁ

First: _____ קָדוֹשׁ קָדוֹשׁ

_____

יְיָ בָּרוּךְ מִמְּקוֹמוֹ כְּבוֹד

Second: _____

אֱלֹהַיִךְ יְיָ הַלְלוּיָהּ יִמְלֹךְ לְדוֹר וָדוֹר לְעוֹלָם צִיוֹן

Third: _____

_____

_____

Can you recite each response by heart?

The קְדוּשָׁה is recited by the leader of the prayer service.

Four verses in the קְדוּשָׁה connect the congregational responses.

First Verse: lines 4-6

Write the first three words _____ _____ _____

Write the last five words _____ _____ _____

_____ _____

The root of the first word is ___ ___ ___

One other word in the verse with this root: _____

ך is a suffix.

ך means _____, _____, _____.

Write the two words in the verse that contain the suffix ך.

_____ _____

Second Verse: lines 9-11

Write the first three words: _____ _____ _____

Write the last three words: _____ _____ _____

There are many words with two, three and four letters in the verse.

two-letters; _____

three-letters: _____

four-letters: _____

Third Verse: lines 13-18

Write the first five words: _____ _____

_____ _____ _____

Write the last five words: _____ _____

_____ _____ _____

Many words in this verse are written with a final letter.

Write the final form of each letter:

נ ___ מ ___ צ ___ כב ___ פפ ___

Lightly circle each final letter in the verse.

Write each of the circled words in the correct column.

ך	ם	ן
_____	_____	_____
_____	_____	_____
_____	_____	
_____		
_____		
_____		
_____		
_____		

FAMILIAR PRAYER WORDS

In lines 13-18 you read words found in many prayers passages.

לְעוֹלָם וָעֶד	מָשִׁיחַ	צִיּוֹן	יְרוּשָׁלַיִם
forever	anointed (Messiah)	Zion	Jerusalem

דָוִד	מַלְכֵּנוּ	לְדוֹר וָדוֹר
David	our King	unto all generations

Write the Hebrew:

our King _____

Zion _____

forever _____

Jerusalem _____

unto all generations _____

David _____

anointed (Messiah) _____

Can you read the Hebrew words without a mistake?

Can you read the English and say each Hebrew word by heart?

קְדוּשַׁת הַשֵּׁם

An important root in the verse is מ-ל-ךְ.

מ-ל-ךְ means "king".

Write the root: ____ ____ ____

Remember: Final ךְ is part of a family of letters.

Write the family members here: _____ _____ _____

Write the English sound for each: _____ _____ _____

Write the four words in the verse that are built on the root מ-ל-ךְ.

_____

━━━━━━━ READING CHALLENGE ━━━━━━━

Can you read lines 19-20 without a mistake?

Can you read lines 4-20 without a mistake?

Fourth Verse: The conclusion to the קְדוּשָׁה is found on lines 21-24.

Write the first four words _____ _____ _____ _____

The phrase לְדוֹר וָדוֹר appears three times in the קְדוּשָׁה.

Find and lightly underline the phrase in lines 16, 19 and 21.

Add the vowels to complete the Hebrew:

Line 16-17 לדור ודור ולנצח נצחים

Line 19-20 אלהיך ציון לדור ודור הללויה

Line 21-22 לדור ודור נגיד גדלך ולנצח נצחים
קדשתך נקדיש

קְדוּשַׁת הַשֵׁם

Can you find and write the following:

the words in the fourth verse built on the root ק־ד־שׁ

_____

the words with the final letter ך

_____

the word meaning "our God" _____

the phrase meaning "forever" _____

the final sentence of the קְדוּשָׁה

_____

Write the names of the first three בְּרָכוֹת in the עֲמִידָה

_____

_____

_____

Write: the Hebrew word for "fathers" _____

the Hebrew word for "our fathers" _____

the Hebrew and English names of our fathers:

_____   _____

_____   _____

_____   _____

34

Write: the Hebrew word meaning "powers" _____

Write the Hebrew phrases:

"upholds the falling" _____

"and heals the sick" _____

"and keeps faith with those who sleep in the dust"

_____

Write: the term meaning "the holiness of God" _____

the root meaning "holy" ___ ___ ___

the words missing from the third בְּרָכָה: קְדוּשַׁת הַשֵׁם

וּשְׁמְךָ _____ אַתָּה _____

סֶלָה. _____ בְּכָל־יוֹם _____

_____ _____, _____ בָּרוּךְ אַתָּה

the words missing from these congregational responses

found in the קְדוּשָׁה.

יְיָ צְבָאוֹת, _____ _____ קָדוֹשׁ

_____ _____ מְלֹא

_____ _____ בָּרוּךְ כְּבוֹד

_____ לְעוֹלָם, _____ יִמְלֹךְ

_____, לְדוֹר _____

Complete the final sentence of קְדוּשַׁת הַשֵׁם.

_____ בָּרוּךְ

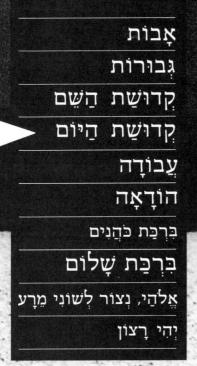
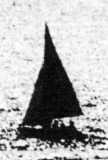

This בְּרָכָה is recited only in the morning עֲמִידָה for Shabbat (on weekdays, the middle section of the עֲמִידָה consists of thirteen blessings). קְדוּשַׁת הַיּוֹם means *sanctification of the day*. To sanctify means *to make holy*. The בְּרָכָה repeats the teaching of the Torah that Shabbat is a sign of the covenant between God and the people Israel. God, who gave the holy Sabbath to us, sanctifies this day, whose holiness we must continue as it sustains us.

קְדוּשַׁת הַיּוֹם

1 יִשְׂמַח מֹשֶׁה בְּמַתְּנַת חֶלְקוֹ, כִּי עֶבֶד נֶאֱמָן

2 קָרָאתָ לּוֹ. כְּלִיל תִּפְאֶרֶת בְּרֹאשׁוֹ נָתַתָּ, בְּעָמְדוֹ

3 לְפָנֶיךָ עַל הַר סִינַי וּשְׁנֵי לֻחוֹת אֲבָנִים הוֹרִיד

4 בְּיָדוֹ, וְכָתוּב בָּהֶם שְׁמִירַת שַׁבָּת, וְכֵן כָּתוּב

5 בְּתוֹרָתֶךָ:

וְשָׁמְרוּ בְנֵי יִשְׂרָאֵל אֶת־הַשַּׁבָּת, לַעֲשׂוֹת אֶת־ 6

הַשַּׁבָּת לְדֹרֹתָם בְּרִית עוֹלָם. בֵּינִי וּבֵין בְּנֵי 7

יִשְׂרָאֵל אוֹת הִיא לְעֹלָם, כִּי שֵׁשֶׁת יָמִים עָשָׂה 8

יְיָ אֶת־הַשָּׁמַיִם וְאֶת־הָאָרֶץ, וּבַיּוֹם הַשְּׁבִיעִי 9

שָׁבַת וַיִּנָּפַשׁ. 10

The children of Israel shall keep the Sabbath, observing the
Sabbath throughout their generations as an everlasting covenant.
It is a sign between Me and the children of Israel forever that in
six days the Lord made the heavens and the earth, and on the
seventh day He ceased from work and rested.

Exodus 31:16,17

וְלֹא נְתַתּוֹ, יְיָ אֱלֹהֵינוּ, לְגוֹיֵי הָאֲרָצוֹת, וְלֹא 11

הִנְחַלְתּוֹ, מַלְכֵּנוּ, לְעוֹבְדֵי פְסִילִים, וְגַם 12

בִּמְנוּחָתוֹ לֹא יִשְׁכְּנוּ עֲרֵלִים, כִּי לְיִשְׂרָאֵל עַמְּךָ 13

נְתַתּוֹ בְּאַהֲבָה, לְזֶרַע יַעֲקֹב אֲשֶׁר בָּם בָּחָרְתָּ, 14

עַם מְקַדְּשֵׁי שְׁבִיעִי, כֻּלָּם יִשְׂבְּעוּ וְיִתְעַנְּגוּ 15

מִטּוּבֶךָ. וְהַשְּׁבִיעִי רָצִיתָ בּוֹ וְקִדַּשְׁתּוֹ, חֶמְדַּת 16

יָמִים אוֹתוֹ קָרֵאתָ, זֵכֶר לְמַעֲשֵׂה בְרֵאשִׁית. 17

18 אֱלֹהֵינוּ וֵאלֹהֵי אֲבוֹתֵינוּ, רְצֵה בִמְנוּחָתֵנוּ.

19 קַדְּשֵׁנוּ בְּמִצְוֺתֶיךָ וְתֵן חֶלְקֵנוּ בְּתוֹרָתֶךָ, שַׂבְּעֵנוּ

20 מִטּוּבֶךָ וְשַׂמְּחֵנוּ בִּישׁוּעָתֶךָ, וְטַהֵר לִבֵּנוּ לְעָבְדְּךָ

21 בֶּאֱמֶת. וְהַנְחִילֵנוּ, יְיָ אֱלֹהֵינוּ, בְּאַהֲבָה וּבְרָצוֹן

22 שַׁבַּת קָדְשֶׁךָ, וְיָנוּחוּ בָהּ יִשְׂרָאֵל מְקַדְּשֵׁי שְׁמֶךָ.

Our God and God of our fathers, be pleased with our rest. Make
us holy through Your commandments and set our portion among
those who devote themselves to Your Torah. Satisfy us with Your
goodness and make us rejoice in Your deliverance. Purify our
hearts to serve You in truth. O Lord our God, cause us to enjoy
in love the heritage of Your holy Sabbath; and may the people of
Israel who sanctify Your name, find true rest on this day.

23 בָּרוּךְ אַתָּה יְיָ, מְקַדֵּשׁ הַשַּׁבָּת.

Blessed are You, O Lord who sanctifies the Sabbath.

קְדוּשַׁת הַיּוֹם is recited only on _Shabat_____.

קְדוּשַׁת הַיּוֹם means _____.

"to sanctify" means _____.

The Hebrew root for "holy" is קָדֹשׁ___ ____

This root is found in the name of the בְּרָכָה.

Write each word built on the root קָ־דָ־שׁ _____

line 15 ___ מְקַדֵּשׁ___ line 16 ____ קִדַּשְׁתָּ _____

line 19 _____ קְדוּשָׁה _____

line 22 ____ קְדֻשַּׁת ___ ___ " ___

line 23 _____ קִדְּשׁוֹ _____

Which word is repeated? ____ קְדוּשַׁת _____

Read each word built on the root קָ־דָ־שׁ.

Read each complete line that contains these words.

40

הַיוֹם means "the day".

The special day the בְּרָכָה speaks about is Shabbat — שַׁבָּת.

Write the Hebrew word for Shabbat: _____

שׁ־ב־ת is an important root.

שׁ־ב־ת means "to cease from work".

Lightly circle each word built on the root שׁ־ב־ת: lines 4, 6, 7, 10,

22, 23

Write the word circled on line 10: _____

"and He ceased from work".

Write the common root letters: שַׁבָּת שָׁבַת

_____

Read the phrases מְקַדֵּשׁ הַשַׁבָּת and שַׁבַּת קָדְשֶׁךָ.

Lightly circle the root meaning "holy" in each phrase.

Lightly circle each word meaning "a day of rest".

Complete the final sentence in the בְּרָכָה.

בָּרוּךְ _____

This sentence has been translated for you.

Write the translation here:

_____

יְהֹוָה	בְּנֵי יִשְׂרָאֵל	לְעוֹלָם	יִשְׂרָאֵל
God	children of Israel	forever everlasting	Israel

שַׁבָּת	זֵכֶר	מֹשֶׁה	הַשָּׁמַיִם	הָאָרֶץ
Sabbath	remembrance	Moses	the heaven	the earth

מַלְכֵּנוּ	בֶּאֱמֶת	יְיָ	בְּרֵאשִׁית	יַעֲקֹב
our King	in truth	God	creation	Jacob

אֱלֹהֵינוּ וֵאלֹהֵי אֲבוֹתֵינוּ	לְדֹרֹתָם
our God and God of our fathers	throughout their generations

Can you read each KEY WORD without a mistake?

Can you read the Hebrew and give the English meaning by heart?

אֱלֹהֵינוּ וֵאלֹהֵי אֲבוֹתֵינוּ

The phrase is found at the beginning of **אָבוֹת**.

Write the meaning: _____

The phrase begins the final paragraph of **קְדוּשַׁת הַיּוֹם**

(lines 18-22).

Lightly underline it in the passage.

Write the phrase: _____

Our forefathers were Abraham, Isaac and Jacob.

Write the Hebrew name found in the Key Words: _____

Write the other two names in Hebrew: _____ _____

God's name is found twice in the Key Words.

Write each name: _____ _____

God is "our King".

Write the Hebrew: _____

The word אֱמֶת is often found in prayers.

Write the KEY WORD meaning "in truth": _____

Find this word in line 21.

Add the vowels to complete the phrase (beginning on line 20):

וטהר לבנו לעבדך בֶּאֱמֶת

Israel is the homeland of the Jewish people.

Write Israel in Hebrew: _____

The Jewish people are called the "children of Israel".

Write the Hebrew phrase: _____

Moses led the children of Israel from Egypt.

Write his name in Hebrew. _____

לְדוֹר וָדוֹר means "to all generations".

Write the Hebrew word meaning "throughout their generations":

_____

Add the vowels to complete the phrase (beginning on line 6):

לעשות את השבת לְדֹרֹתָם ברית עולם

Write the Hebrew word found in the KEY WORD list meaning

"everlasting", "forever". _____

Write the two-word phrase meaning "forever": לְ _____ וָ _____

This passage talks about the "day of rest" given to the Jewish people.

The Hebrew for this special day is _____

Write the Hebrew word meaning "the earth": _____

Write the Hebrew word meaning "the heaven": _____

Add the vowels to complete the Hebrew (beginning on line 8):

כִּי שֵׁשֶׁת יָמִים עָשָׂה יי אֶת הַשָּׁמַיִם וְאֶת
הָאָרֶץ, וּבַיּוֹם הַשְּׁבִיעִי שָׁבַת וַיִּנָּפַשׁ.

"for in six days the Lord made heaven and earth, and on the seventh

day He ceased from work and rested".

God made the seventh day a holy day "in remembrance of creation".

Write the Hebrew word meaning "remembrance": _____

Write the Hebrew word meaning "creation": _____

Find each word in line 17. Lightly circle each.

Add the vowels to complete the Hebrew (found in line 17):

זֵכֶר לְמַעֲשֵׂה בְרֵאשִׁית

READING CHALLENGE

Can you read lines 6-10 without a mistake?

MEMORY CHALLENGE

Study the KEY WORDS.

Can you read the English and supply the Hebrew word by heart?

קְדוּשַׁת הַיּוֹם

The suffix ךְ and the suffix נוּ are often found in קְדוּשַׁת הַיּוֹם.

נוּ means "us", "our", "we"

ךְ means _____

Find and lightly circle each of these suffixes in the בְּרָכָה.

Write each of the circled words in the correct column.

ךְ	נוּ
אֶלֹהֵי	עֲבֵךָ
מֶלֶךָ	מִשִׁוּבוּ
מַשׁׁוּבֵדוֹ	הַמַעֲרָׁוֹתוּ
לֹוֹחֵם	פַּתוֹתֵנוּ
אֲבוֹתֵיךָ	מַחַיָבֵד
בִּתוֹתֶוָּהָ	בְּשִׁמְאָתֶךָ
לְֹדֵשׁוֹתוּ	לְעָבִדֵךָ
תַחֲלַקֵךָ	קִדִשׁוֹבֵ
נָתַֹעֲרַבִ	הֵישׁוּבַךָ
לְשִׁמְתָחֵםֹ	בִּבְרַחֲתֵיוַ
לְֹהֵוֹ	חֵלֵקַוֹ
	שִׁוֹלֵבַךָ
	רֵשׁׁוֹתֵבַ
	לְבִוּ
	רַהַבְהוֹלֵנַ
	לְעָרָשֵׁת

FINALS

Complete the lists.

Words in the בְּרָכָה with final ם:

אַרְנ־ית	בַּהֶם	עַמּוֹ	קְדוֹשָׁה	־
line 3	line 4	line 7	line 7	line 8

עַלְם	רַבִּים	הַשָּׁעִים	וַדָם	בְּטֵלִים
line 8	line 9	line 9	line 12	line 12

שַׁבְּתוֹ	ם	עַם	יוֹם	רַעֲזֹת
line 13	line 14	line 15	line 15	line 17

Words in the בְּרָכָה with final ן:

רַעֲץ	וַד	דְבָרֶיךָ	וְתֵךְ	וְרֵצַן
line 1	line 4	line 7	line 19	line 21

READING CHALLENGE

Can you read lines 18-22 without a mistake?

SINGING CHALLENGE

The second paragraph in קְדוּשַׁת הַיוֹם is often sung. (lines 6-10)

Can you learn to sing וְשָׁמְרוּ?

47

קְדוּשַׁת הַיוֹם

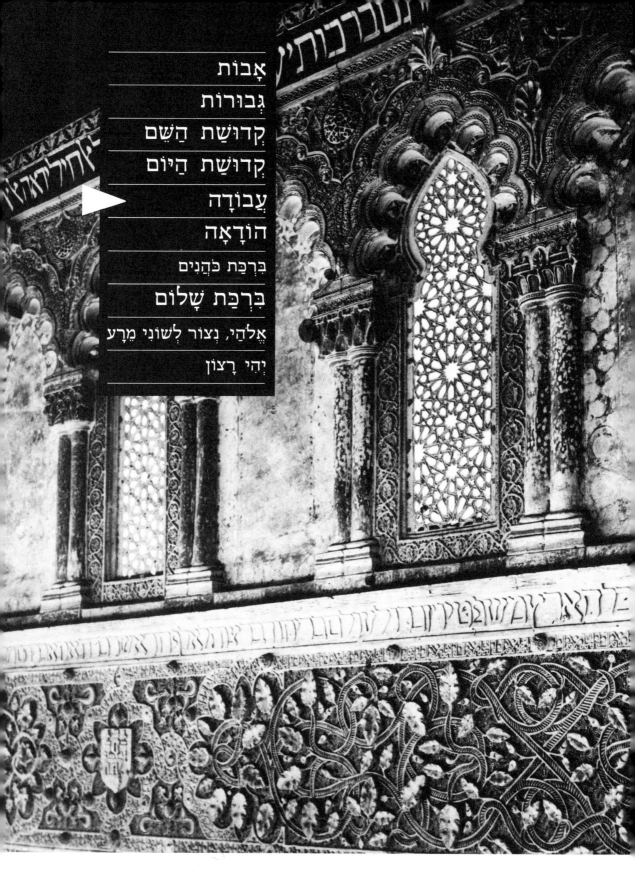

The last three blessings in every עֲמִידָה are always the same. עֲבוֹדָה is the first of these final three blessings. In this blessing עֲבוֹדָה means *worship*. We ask God to accept the prayers — the worship — of our people. The בְּרָכָה also recalls the Temple in ancient Jerusalem.

עֲבוֹדָה

1 רְצֵה יְיָ אֱלֹהֵינוּ בְּעַמְּךָ יִשְׂרָאֵל וּבִתְפִלָּתָם,

2 וְהָשֵׁב אֶת־הָעֲבוֹדָה לִדְבִיר בֵּיתֶךָ (וְאִשֵּׁי

3 יִשְׂרָאֵל) וּתְפִלָּתָם בְּאַהֲבָה תְקַבֵּל בְּרָצוֹן, וּתְהִי

4 לְרָצוֹן תָּמִיד עֲבֹדַת יִשְׂרָאֵל עַמֶּךָ. וְתֶחֱזֶינָה

5 עֵינֵינוּ בְּשׁוּבְךָ לְצִיּוֹן בְּרַחֲמִים.

Look with favor, Lord our God, on Your people Israel and their prayer. Restore worship to Your Temple. Accept with favor (the offerings and) the prayer of the people Israel presented lovingly. May the worship of Your people Israel always find favor with You. May our eyes witness Your return to Zion in mercy.

בָּרוּךְ אַתָּה יְיָ, הַמַּחֲזִיר שְׁכִינָתוֹ לְצִיּוֹן.

Blessed are You, O Lord who restores His presence to Zion.

עֲבוֹדָה asks God to favorably accept the prayer (תְּפִלָּה) and the

worship (עֲבוֹדָה) of our people.

ע־ב־ד is an important root in this passage.

ע־ב־ד means "worship".

Write the root: ע ב ד

Lightly circle the two words in the בְּרָכָה built on the root ע־ב־ד.

Write each: הָעֲבוֹדָה עֲבֹד

The root פ־ל־ל means "pray" or "prayer".

Write the root: פ ל ל

Write the Hebrew word meaning "prayer": _____

One root letter is not found in the word for "prayer": ___

Lightly circle the two words in the בְּרָכָה built on the root פ־ל־ל.

Write each: _____ וּתְפִלָּתָם

"Your people Israel" is a phrase found twice in the passage

בְּעַמְּךָ יִשְׂרָאֵל   יִשְׂרָאֵל עַמֶּךָ

Write each phrase here: בְּעַמְּךָ יִשְׂרָאֵל

יִשְׂרָאֵל עַמֶּךָ

עֲבוֹדָה asks God to:

רְצֵה יְיָ אֱלֹהֵינוּ בְּעַמְּךָ יִשְׂרָאֵל וּבִתְפִלָּתָם

"Look with favor, Lord our God, on Your people Israel and

their prayer."

וּתְהִי לְרָצוֹן תָּמִיד עֲבֹדַת יִשְׂרָאֵל עַמֶּךָ

"May the worship of Your people Israel always find favor with You."

Write the phrases:

"on your people Israel and their prayers" _____

_____

"the worship of your people Israel" _____

_____

צִיּוֹן — "Zion" is the land of Israel.

Find and lightly circle the word צִיּוֹן each time it appears

in the בְּרָכָה.

Write the word as it appears. _____ "to Zion"

Copy each sentence that contains the word צִיּוֹן:

וְתֶחֱזֶינָה _____

בָּרוּךְ _____

_____

Circle the three words that show that בְּרָכָה is a עֲבוֹדָה.

FINAL LETTERS

Write the five final Hebrew letters: ך ן ץ ם ף

Find each word with a final letter in עֲבוֹדָה.

Write each word in the correct column.

ן	ם	ר
הָרָצוֹן	וְנִבְלַעְתָּ	כְּמֹה
לְעוֹלָם	וְתָבֹאתָה	בֵּיתֶךָ
צִיּוֹן	בָּרֶחֶם	עֵינֶיךָ
לְצִיּוֹן		בָּרוּךְ
		בְּעֶרְבָּה

Which word with final ן appears twice in the בְּרָכָה?

דָּגֵשׁ: A SPECIAL DOT

A דָּגֵשׁ is a special dot found in the middle of a letter.

Sometimes the דָּגֵשׁ changes the sound of the letter.

כ כ פ פ בּ ב

Many times the דָּגֵשׁ does not change the sound of the letter.

Find each word with a דָּגֵשׁ in עֲבוֹדָה and write it here:

_____   _____   _____

_____   _____   _____

_____   _____   _____

_____   _____   _____

_____   _____   _____

                                          _____

מֶתֶג: A SPECIAL ACCENT MARK

A Hebrew word is usually accented on the last syllable.

The accent mark tells you to accent a different syllable.

It is usually placed to the left of the vowel: ֵ֛ ֵ֛ ָ֛

Find each word in עֲבוֹדָה with an accent mark and write them here:

_____   _____   _____

_____   _____

God's name is written in different ways.

יְיָ   יְהֹוָה   אֵל   אֱלֹהִים   אֱלֹהֵי   אֲדֹנָי   <u>שכינה</u>

יְיָ is read twice in the **בְּרָכָה**.

Add the vowels to complete the phrases:

רְצֵה   יְיָ   אלהינו

בָּרוּךְ   אתה   יְיָ

The Hebrew word meaning "Divine Presence" is **שְׁכִינָה**.

שְׁכִינָה is another way of referring to God.

Write the Hebrew word: <u>שְׁכִינָה</u>

Add it to the list of God's names.

Find the word in the concluding sentence of **עֲבוֹדָה** that means "His Divine Presence".

Write the word here: <u>שְׁכִינָתוֹ</u>

Complete the final sentence:

בָּרוּךְ אַתָּה יְיָ _____

READING CHALLENGE

Can you read the entire בְּרָכָה without a mistake?

MEMORY CHALLENGE

Can you recite the final sentence by heart?

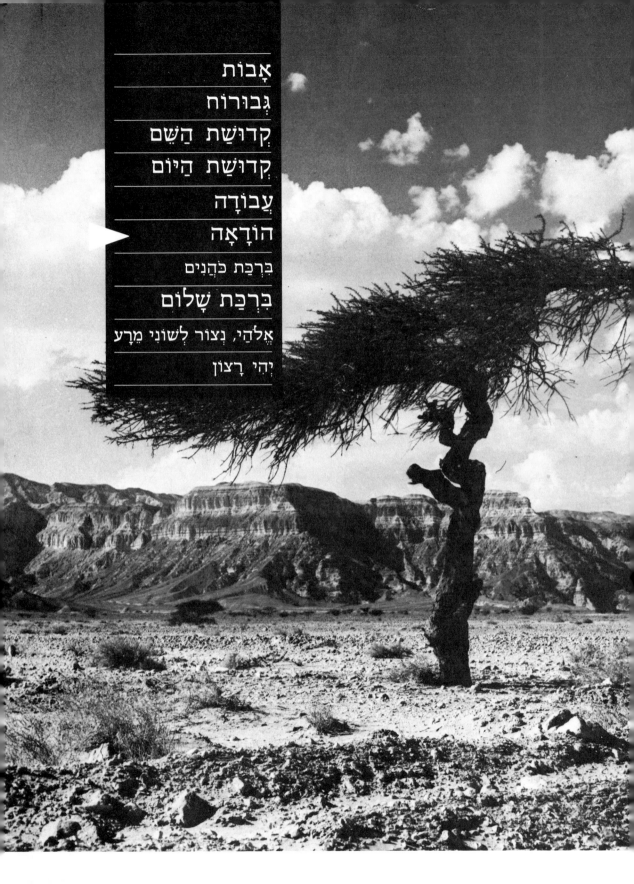

הוֹדָאָה is a blessing of acknowledgment and thanksgiving. It is the second of the final three blessings of the עֲמִידָה. We acknowledge God as the creator of all things and we thank God for His daily miracles. The beginning of this בְּרָכָה has two versions. The first passage below is said by members of the congregation reciting the עֲמִידָה silently. During the repetition of the עֲמִידָה, the leader chants the first passage aloud while the congregation recites the second one silently.

הוֹדָאָה

1 מוֹדִים אֲנַחְנוּ לָךְ, שָׁאַתָּה הוּא יְיָ אֱלֹהֵינוּ

2 וֵאלֹהֵי אֲבוֹתֵינוּ לְעוֹלָם וָעֶד, צוּר חַיֵּינוּ, מָגֵן

3 יִשְׁעֵנוּ אַתָּה הוּא לְדוֹר וָדוֹר. נוֹדֶה לְךָ וּנְסַפֵּר

4 תְּהִלָּתֶךָ, עַל חַיֵּינוּ הַמְּסוּרִים בְּיָדֶךָ, וְעַל

5 נִשְׁמוֹתֵינוּ הַפְּקוּדוֹת לָךְ, וְעַל נִסֶּיךָ שֶׁבְּכָל-יוֹם

6 עִמָּנוּ, וְעַל נִפְלְאוֹתֶיךָ וְטוֹבוֹתֶיךָ שֶׁבְּכָל-עֵת,

7 עֶרֶב וָבֹקֶר וְצָהֳרָיִם. הַטּוֹב כִּי לֹא כָלוּ רַחֲמֶיךָ,

8 וְהַמְרַחֵם כִּי לֹא תַמּוּ חֲסָדֶיךָ, מֵעוֹלָם קִוִּינוּ לָךְ.

57

⁹ וְעַל כֻּלָּם יִתְבָּרַךְ וְיִתְרוֹמַם שִׁמְךָ מַלְכֵּנוּ תָּמִיד

¹⁰ לְעוֹלָם וָעֶד. וְכֹל הַחַיִּים יוֹדוּךָ סֶּלָה, וִיהַלְלוּ

¹¹ אֶת־שִׁמְךָ בֶּאֱמֶת, הָאֵל יְשׁוּעָתֵנוּ וְעֶזְרָתֵנוּ סֶלָה.

For all this, our King, shall Your name be praised and exalted forever. Every living creature shall thank you always and shall praise Your name in truth. O God, You are our deliverance and our help.

¹² בָּרוּךְ אַתָּה יְיָ, הַטּוֹב שִׁמְךָ וּלְךָ נָאֶה לְהוֹדוֹת.

Blessed are You, O Lord who is all good and to whom it is fitting to offer praise.

During the repetition of the עֲמִידָה aloud, the leader chants the preceding passage while the congregation recites this passage silently.

13 מוֹדִים אֲנַחְנוּ לָךְ, שָׁאַתָּה הוּא יְיָ אֱלֹהֵינוּ

14 וֵאלֹהֵי אֲבוֹתֵינוּ, אֱלֹהֵי כָל־בָּשָׂר, יוֹצְרֵנוּ יוֹצֵר

15 בְּרֵאשִׁית, בְּרָכוֹת וְהוֹדָאוֹת לְשִׁמְךָ הַגָּדוֹל

16 וְהַקָּדוֹשׁ, עַל שֶׁהֶחֱיִיתָנוּ וְקִיַּמְתָּנוּ. כֵּן תְּחַיֵּנוּ

17 וּתְקַיְּמֵנוּ וְתֶאֱסֹף גָּלֻיּוֹתֵינוּ לְחַצְרוֹת קָדְשֶׁךָ,

18 לִשְׁמֹר חֻקֶּיךָ וְלַעֲשׂוֹת רְצוֹנֶךָ וּלְעָבְדְּךָ בְּלֵבָב

19 שָׁלֵם עַל שֶׁאֲנַחְנוּ מוֹדִים לָךְ. בָּרוּךְ אֵל

20 הַהוֹדָאוֹת.

59

הוֹדָאָה is a בְּרָכָה of thanksgiving.

Find and lightly circle each word in lines 12, 15 and 20

related to הוֹדָאָה.

Write each word here: _____ _____

_____

Look at the first passage of הוֹדָאָה (lines 1-8).

Look at the second version of הוֹדָאָה (lines 13-20).

Lightly underline the phrase introducing each passage:

מוֹדִים אֲנַחְנוּ לָךְ

Copy the phrase: _____

"We thankfully acknowledge"

Add the vowels to complete the introductory words found in both

passages:

מודים אנחנו לך, שאתה הוא יי אלהינו
ואלהי אבותינו

"We thankfully acknowledge that You are the Lord our God and God

of our fathers".

The passage speaks to "our God and God of our fathers".

Write the words in Hebrew: _____

Each passage concludes with the same words.

Fill in the missing words.

9 וְעַל כֻּלָם _____ _____

_____ _____ תָּמִיד

10 _____ _____. וְכֹל

_____ _____ סֶלָה,

_____

11 אֶת _____ _____ , הָאֵל

_____ _____ סֶלָה

12 בָּרוּךְ אַתָּה יְיָ, ___ _____

_____ _____ וּלְךָ .

Circle the three words that tell us that הַהוֹדָאָה is a בְּרָכָה.

This sentence has been translated for you.

Write the meaning here:

_____

_____

KEY WORDS TO READ AND UNDERSTAND

These words are found in lines 1-8 and 17-20.

קֻוִּינוּ	עִמָּנוּ	נִשְׁמוֹתֵינוּ	יִשְׁעֵנוּ	חַיֵּינוּ
we hope	with us	our souls	saves us	our lives

אֱלֹהֵינוּ	וְעֶזְרָתֵנוּ	יְשׁוּעָתֵנוּ	מַלְכֵּנוּ
our God	our help	our salvation	our King

נִפְלְאוֹתֶיךָ	בְּיָדֶךָ	תְּהִלָּתֶךָ	לָךְ לְךָ	נִסֶּיךָ
Your wonders	Your hand	Your praise	to You	Your miracles

יוֹדוּךָ	שְׁמֶךָ	רַחֲמֶיךָ	וְטוֹבוֹתֶיךָ	חֲסָדֶיךָ
honor You	Your name	Your mercy	Your goodness	Your loving kindness

Each Key Word ends with the suffix ךָ or נוּ.

ךָ means _____

נוּ means _____

Write each Key Word with the suffix **ךָ.**

Your praise _____

Your hand _____

Your miracles _____

Your wonders _____

Your goodness _____

Your mercy _____

Your loving-kindness _____

Your name _____

honor You _____

to you _____

Write each KEY WORD with the suffix **נוּ.**

our God _____

our lives _____

our souls _____

our King _____

our help _____

our salvation _____

with us _____

saves us _____

we hope _____

━━━ **MORE KEY WORDS TO READ AND UNDERSTAND** ━━━

Many words in lines 13-20 also end with the suffix ךְ or נוּ.

Read each of these KEY WORDS.

Find and read the words that end with a final letter.

יוֹצְרֵנוּ	וְקִיַּמְתָּנוּ	תְּחַיֵּנוּ
our Creator	and sustained us	keep us in life

וּתְקַיְּמֵנוּ	כֵּן	שֶׁהֶחֱיִיתָנוּ
and sustain us	continue to	You have kept us in life

וְתֶאֱסֹף	בְּלֵבָב שָׁלֵם	רְצֹנֶךָ	וְלַעֲשׂוֹת
and gather	with a perfect heart	Your will	and to do

חֻקֶּיךָ	גָּלִיּוֹתֵינוּ	לִשְׁמֹר	וּלְעָבְדְּךָ
Your statutes	our exiles	to observe	and to serve You

UNDERSTAND THE CONNECTION

Write the Hebrew on the line above the English.

_____   _____

and sustained us   You have kept us in life

_____   _____   _____

and sustain us   keep us in life   continue to

_____   _____   _____   _____

Your statutes   to observe   our exiles   and gather

_____   _____   _____   _____

with a perfect heart   and to serve You   Your will   and to do

You have written phrases that appear in the בְּרָכָה.

Can you find and read them in the passage?

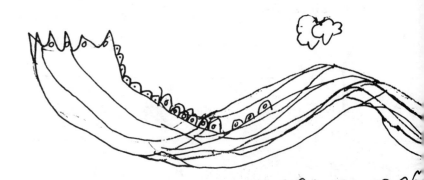

הוֹדָאָה

Find each word in the בְּרָכָה with an מֶתֶג and write it in the space provided.

Lines 1-8

1 _____ _____

2 _____ _____

3 _____

4 _____ _____

_____

5 _____ _____

6 _____ _____

_____

7 _____ _____

_____ _____

8 _____ _____

_____

Lines 13-20

13 _____ _____

14 _____ _____

16 _____ _____

_____ _____

17 _____ _____

_____ _____

18 _____ _____

19 _____

Concluding lines 9-12

9 _____ _____

10 _____ _____

11 _____ _____

_____

Which word was found in lines 10 and 11?

_____

This word is not translated into English.

It can mean "forever" or "halleluyah".

READING CHALLENGE

Can you read each accented word correctly?

Can you now read each passage without a mistake?

Can you read both עֲבוֹדָה and הוֹדָאָה easily?

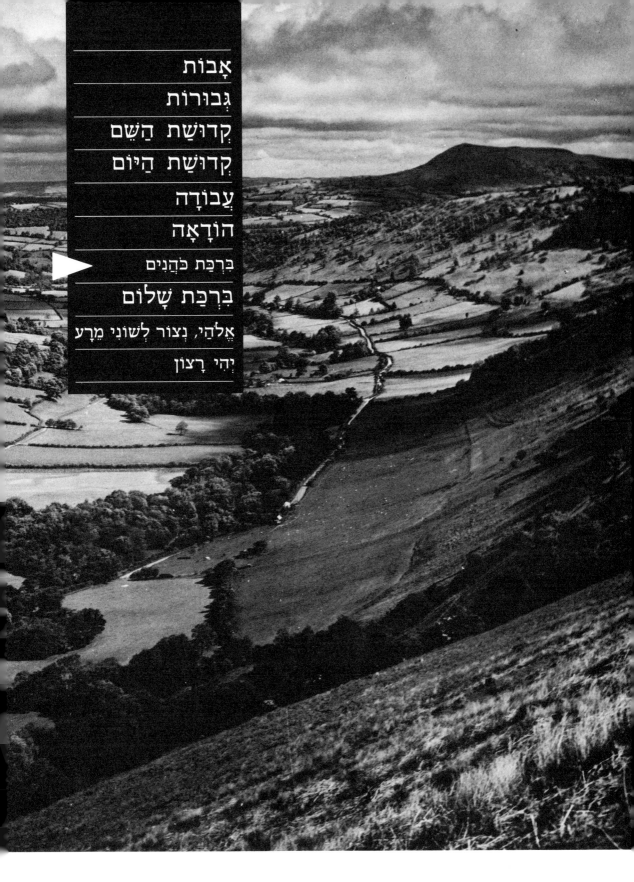

בִּרְכַּת כֹּהֲנִים is added when the leader repeats the עֲמִידָה aloud. It is not one of the blessings of the עֲמִידָה. בִּרְכַּת כֹּהֲנִים is the *Priestly Blessing*. It is found in the Torah, in the Book of Numbers 6:24-26. כֹּהֲנִים were members of the priestly tribe in ancient Israel. They gave God's blessing to the people during the service in the Temple in ancient Jerusalem. These same words are recited by the leader of our service, who need not be a *kohen*.

בִּרְכַּת כֹּהֲנִים

1 אֱלֹהֵינוּ וֵאלֹהֵי אֲבוֹתֵינוּ, בָּרְכֵנוּ בַּבְּרָכָה
2 הַמְשֻׁלֶּשֶׁת, בַּתּוֹרָה הַכְּתוּבָה עַל יְדֵי מֹשֶׁה
3 עַבְדֶּךָ, הָאֲמוּרָה מִפִּי אַהֲרֹן וּבָנָיו, כֹּהֲנִים, עַם
4 קְדוֹשֶׁךָ, כָּאָמוּר:

Our God and God of our fathers, bless us with the threefold blessing written in the Torah by Your servant Moses, and spoken by the priests, Aaron and his descendants, Your holy people:

69

Congregation responds:

כֵּן יְהִי רָצוֹן.   יְבָרֶכְךָ יְיָ וְיִשְׁמְרֶךָ.

כֵּן יְהִי רָצוֹן.   יָאֵר יְיָ פָּנָיו אֵלֶיךָ וִיחֻנֶּךָּ.

יִשָּׂא יְיָ פָּנָיו אֵלֶיךָ וְיָשֵׂם לְךָ שָׁלוֹם.

כֵּן יְהִי רָצוֹן.

May the Lord bless you and keep you.
May the Lord show you favor and be gracious unto you.
May the Lord show you kindness and give you peace.

Congregation responds:

May this be His will.

May this be His will.

May this be His will.

70

בִּרְכַּת כֹּהֲנִים

In Hebrew the Priestly Blessing is called _____ .

Copy the first three words of the passage here:

_____

Translate the three words into English:

_____

Look at lines 5-7.

Which word is found in each line? _____

Copy the three-word phrase found in both lines 6 and 7:

_____

The congregation responds to each blessing.

Copy the response here: _____

Write the English translation: _____

Read בִּרְכַּת כֹּהֲנִים.

Fill in the missing words in each blessing.

Fill in the missing words in each response.

יְיָ _____ •_____

כֵּן יְהִי _____•

יָאֵר _____ _____

וִיחֻנֶּךָ• _____

כֵּן _____ _____•

יִשָּׂא _____ _____ _____

וְיָשֵׂם לְךָ _____•

_____ _____ _____•

READING CHALLENGE

Can you read each blessing and the response without a mistake?

בִּרְכַּת כֹּהֲנִים

AN IMPORTANT ROOT

בּ־ר־ך is an important root.

בּ־ר־ך means "bless" or "praise".

Write the root: ＿＿ ＿＿ ＿＿

Write the words in lines 1 and 5 built on the root בּ־ר־ך:

_____

Write the name of the passage in Hebrew:

_____

Circle the root letters in בִּרְכַּת.

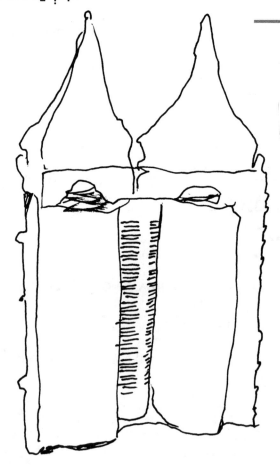

בִּרְכַּת כֹּהֲנִים

These words are found in lines 1-4.

Find the Hebrew word in the passage. Write it next to the English

word.

our God _____   and the God

in the Torah _____   of _____

our fathers _____   Moses _____

bless us _____   priests _____

Your holy   Aaron _____

   people _____   blessing _____

Fill in the missing words.

אֱלֹהֵינוּ _____ _____, _____

עַל _____ _____ _____ הַמְשֻׁלֶּשֶׁת, _____

_____ מִפִּי _____ עַבְדֶּךָ, _____ יְדֵי

כָּאָמוּר: _____ עִם _____ _____,

Can you read the Priestly Blessing correctly?

Can the class respond in the appropriate place?

Can you re-write the Priestly Blessing in the correct order?

יָאֵר יְיָ פָּנָיו אֵלֶיךָ וִיחֻנֶּךָ.

יִשָּׂא יְיָ פָּנָיו אֵלֶיךָ וְיָשֵׂם לְךָ שָׁלוֹם.

יְבָרֶכְךָ יְיָ וְיִשְׁמְרֶךָ.

_____ 1

_____ 2

_____ 3

בִּרְכַּת כֹּהֲנִים

אָבוֹת

גְּבוּרוֹת

קְדוּשַׁת הַשֵּׁם

קְדוּשַׁת הַיּוֹם

עֲבוֹדָה

הוֹדָאָה

בִּרְכַּת כֹּהֲנִים

◀ בִּרְכַּת שָׁלוֹם

אֱלֹהַי, נְצוֹר לְשׁוֹנִי מֵרָע

יְהִי רָצוֹן

The final blessing of the עֲמִידָה is called
בִּרְכַּת שָׁלוֹם. It is a prayer for peace. Peace has
always been the most important blessing for the
Jewish people. This בְּרָכָה also includes a prayer
for compassion, and expresses gratitude for Torah,
justice, life and peace.

בִּרְכַּת שָׁלוֹם

1 שִׂים שָׁלוֹם, טוֹבָה וּבְרָכָה, חֵן וָחֶסֶד וְרַחֲמִים

2 עָלֵינוּ וְעַל כָּל יִשְׂרָאֵל עַמֶּךָ. בָּרְכֵנוּ אָבִינוּ כֻּלָּנוּ

3 כְּאֶחָד בְּאוֹר פָּנֶיךָ, כִּי בְאוֹר פָּנֶיךָ נָתַתָּ לָּנוּ, יְיָ

4 אֱלֹהֵינוּ, תּוֹרַת חַיִּים וְאַהֲבַת חֶסֶד, וּצְדָקָה

5 וּבְרָכָה וְרַחֲמִים וְחַיִּים וְשָׁלוֹם. וְטוֹב בְּעֵינֶיךָ

6 לְבָרֵךְ אֶת־עַמְּךָ יִשְׂרָאֵל בְּכָל־עֵת וּבְכָל־שָׁעָה

7 בִּשְׁלוֹמֶךָ.

Grant peace with well-being and blessing,
And grace with lovingkindness and mercy
To us and to all Israel Your people.
Bless us all together with the light of Your presence,
For in that light, Lord our God,
You have given us the Torah of life,
And love of kindness with justice,
Blessing, tenderness, life and peace.
May it be good in Your sight
To bless Your people Israel at all times,
At every hour, with Your peace.
Blessed are You, Lord who blesses His people Israel with peace.

בִּרְכַּת שָׁלוֹם asks for God's blessing of peace — שָׁלוֹם.

Write שָׁלוֹם as it is found on each of these lines:

line 1 _____ line 5 _____

line 7 _____ line 9 _____

The first two words of the blessing asks God to grant peace:

שים שלום

Add the missing vowels.

בִּרְכַּת שָׁלוֹם asks God for the blessing of peace for all the people Israel.

Write the Hebrew word for "Israel": _____

Do you remember the word for "people"? _____

Copy the phrases from the passage which refer to God's people, Israel:

_____ _____ _____

       line 2   line 6   line 8

Lightly underline each of these phrases in the בְּרָכָה.

Many words in the passage are built on the root בּ־ר־ך.

בִּרְכַּת שָׁלוֹם begins with these four words:

_____

Which word is built on the root בּ־ר־ך? _____

Find and write the other words in the blessing built on

the root ‎בּ־ר־ך.

_____	_____	_____	_____	_____
line 2	line 5	line 6	line 8	line 8

‎בִּרְכַּת שָׁלוֹם ends with the three words found at the conclusion of

every ‎בְּרָכָה.

Complete the final sentence:

‎בָּרוּךְ _____

_____

Write the meaning here: _____

_____

KEY WORDS AND PHRASES TO READ AND UNDERSTAND

‎בְּאוֹר פָּנֶיךָ	‎תּוֹרַת חַיִּים	‎וְאַהֲבַת חֶסֶד
with the light of Your Presence	Torah of Life	and love of kindness

‎וּצְדָקָה	‎וּבְרָכָה	‎וְרַחֲמִים	‎וְחַיִּים	‎וְשָׁלוֹם
and justice	and blessing	and mercy	and life	and peace

‎בְּכָל־עֵת	‎וּבְכָל־שָׁעָה
at all times	and at every hour

ANALYZING THE KEY WORDS AND PHRASES

Write the Hebrew phrase "with the light of Your Presence"

_____

The phrase appears twice in line 3 in בִּרְכַּת שָׁלוֹם.

Find and lightly underline it each time.

בִּרְכַּת שָׁלוֹם mentions the blessings God has given to His people,

Israel. Write the Hebrew words above the English translations:

_____   _____   _____

and justice   and love of kindness   Torah of Life

_____   _____   _____   _____

and peace   and life   and mercy   and blessing

Find these words and phrases in בִּרְכַּת שָׁלוֹם (beginning in

line 4).

Lightly underline each phrase.

We ask that we may have the blessing of peace "always".

Write the two phrases:

_____   _____

and at every hour   at all times

SINGING CHALLENGE

Can you learn to sing בִּרְכַּת שָׁלוֹם?

Write the names of the final three בְּרָכוֹת in the עֲמִידָה

_____ _____ _____

Complete the opening sentence of each בְּרָכָה.

Then write the final sentence of each.

רְצֵה _____

_____

Look with favor, Lord our God, on Your people Israel and their prayer.

בָּרוּךְ _____

_____

Blessed are You, O Lord who restores His presence to Zion.

מוֹדִים _____

_____

We thankfully acknowledge that You are the Lord our God and God our fathers to all eternity.

מוֹדִים _____

_____

We thankfully acknowledge that You are the Lord our God, and God of our fathers, God of all that lives.

בָּרוּךְ _____

_____

Blessed are You, O Lord who is all good and to whom it is fitting to offer praise.

שִׂים _____

_____

Grant peace with well-being and blessing, and grace with loving-kindness and mercy to us and to all Israel Your people.

בָּרוּךְ _____

_____

Blessed are You, Lord who blesses His people Israel with peace.

READING CHALLENGE

Can you read each sentence you wrote without a mistake?

Can you now read בִּרְכַּת שָׁלוֹם הוֹדָאָה ,עֲבוֹדָה and fluently?

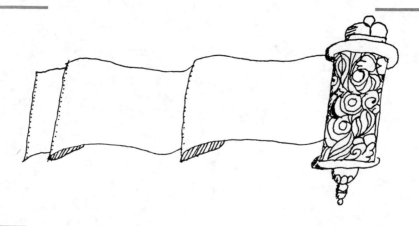

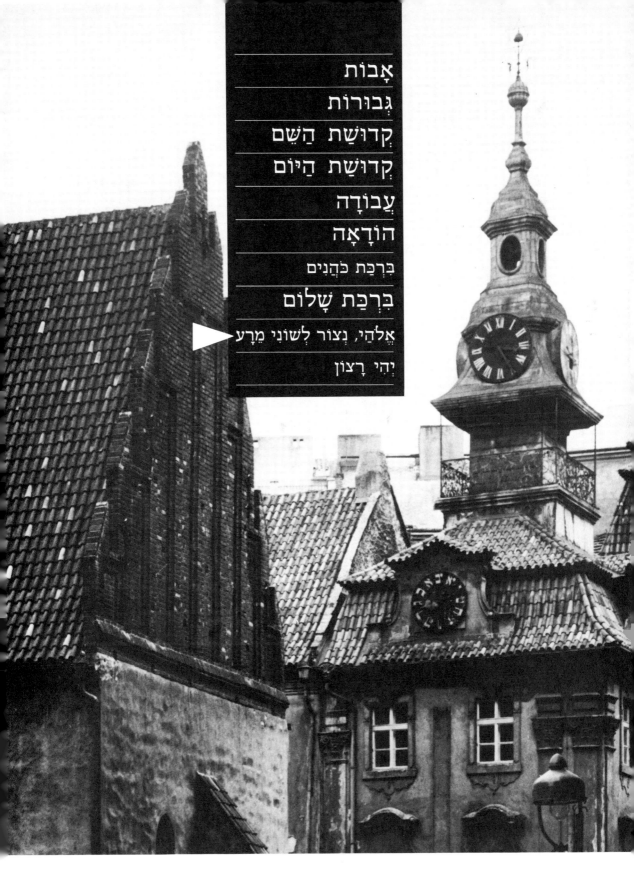

After the concluding blessing of the עֲמִידָה, we add a personal prayer. These words have been adapted from the personal prayer of Mar the son of Ravina, who lived in fourth-century Babylonia. Some of his prayer, found in the Talmud, has become part of our prayer book. The prayer asks God to guide us in our relationships with others, by helping us to control the words we say and to ignore those who speak ill of us. It also asks God's help in opening our heart to His Torah.

אֱלֹהַי, נְצוֹר לְשׁוֹנִי מֵרָע

1 אֱלֹהַי, נְצוֹר לְשׁוֹנִי מֵרָע וּשְׂפָתַי מִדַּבֵּר מִרְמָה.

2 וְלִמְקַלְלַי נַפְשִׁי תִדֹּם, וְנַפְשִׁי כֶּעָפָר לַכֹּל תִּהְיֶה.

3 פְּתַח לִבִּי בְּתוֹרָתֶךָ, וּבְמִצְוֹתֶיךָ תִּרְדֹּף נַפְשִׁי.

4 וְכָל־הַחוֹשְׁבִים עָלַי רָעָה, מְהֵרָה הָפֵר עֲצָתָם

5 וְקַלְקֵל מַחֲשַׁבְתָּם. עֲשֵׂה לְמַעַן שְׁמֶךָ, עֲשֵׂה

85

לְמַעַן יְמִינֶךָ, עֲשֵׂה לְמַעַן קְדֻשָּׁתֶךָ, עֲשֵׂה לְמַעַן 6

תּוֹרָתֶךָ, לְמַעַן יֵחָלְצוּן יְדִידֶיךָ, הוֹשִׁיעָה יְמִינְךָ 7

וַעֲנֵנִי. 8

O Lord, guard my tongue from evil and my lips from speaking falsehood; and to those who slander me, let me give no heed. May my soul be humble and forgiving to all. Open my heart, O Lord, to Your Torah that I may perform Your commandments. As to those who may think evil against me, defeat their aims and undo their purposes, for Your own sake, for Your own power, for Your holiness according to the promise in Your Torah. That Your loved ones be delivered, answer us, O Lord, and save with Your redeeming power.

יִהְיוּ לְרָצוֹן אִמְרֵי־פִי וְהֶגְיוֹן לִבִּי לְפָנֶיךָ, יְיָ 9

צוּרִי וְגֹאֲלִי. 10

May the words of my mouth and the thoughts of my heart be acceptable to You, Lord, my Rock and my Redeemer.

עֹשֶׂה שָׁלוֹם בִּמְרוֹמָיו הוּא יַעֲשֶׂה שָׁלוֹם עָלֵינוּ 11

וְעַל כָּל־יִשְׂרָאֵל, וְאִמְרוּ אָמֵן. 12

May He who ordains peace in the universe bestow peace upon us and upon all the people Israel. Amen.

אֱלֹהַי, נְצוֹר לְשׁוֹנִי מֵרָע

The passage begins: "O Lord, guard my tongue from evil and my lips

from speaking falsehood".

O Lord: אֱלֹהַי

guard my tongue from evil: נְצוֹר לְשׁוֹנִי מֵרָע

and my lips from speaking falsehood: וּשְׂפָתַי מִדַּבֵּר מִרְמָה

and to those who slander me: וְלִמְקַלְלַי

let my soul give no heed: נַפְשִׁי תִדֹּם

May my soul be humble

and forgiving to all: וְנַפְשִׁי כֶּעָפָר לַכֹּל תִּהְיֶה

Open my heart to Your Torah: פְּתַח לִבִּי בְּתוֹרָתֶךָ

that I may perform Your commandments:

וּבְמִצְוֹתֶיךָ תִּרְדֹּף נַפְשִׁי

Fill in the words missing in each phrase.

אֱלֹהַי, נְצוֹר _____ _____

מִרְמָה. _____ _____

וְלִמְקַלְלַי נַפְשִׁי _____ ,

לַכֹּל תִּהְיֶה. _____ _____

פְּתַח _____ _____ ,

נַפְשִׁי. _____ _____

אֱלֹהַי, נְצוֹר לְשׁוֹנִי מֵרָע

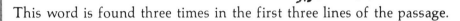

נֶפֶשׁ

נֶפֶשׁ means "soul".

Write the Hebrew: _____

נַפְשִׁי means "my soul".

This word is found three times in the first three lines of the passage.

Find and lightly circle the word.

Can you read the first three lines in the passage without a mistake?

אֱלֹהַי, נְצוֹר לְשׁוֹנִי מֵרָע

AN IMPORTANT ROOT

ע־שׂ־ה is an important root in the passage.

ע־שׂ־ה means "do" or "make".

Write the root: ____ ____ ____

עֲשֵׂה לְמַעַן means "do it for the sake of".

Write the phrase: _____

Find and lightly underline עֲשֵׂה לְמַעַן each time it is read in lines

5 and 6.

Fill in the missing words:

_____ עֲשֵׂה לְמַעַן_____ עֲשֵׂה לְמַעַן

(line 6) Your power   (line 5) your name

_____ עֲשֵׂה לְמַעַן_____ עֲשֵׂה לְמַעַן

(line 7) Your Torah   (line 6) Your holiness

Each word you filled in ends with the suffix _____.

The suffix means _____.

READING CHALLENGE

Practice lines 5-8.

Can you now read lines 1-8 easily?

אֱלֹהַי, נְצוֹר לְשׁוֹנִי מֵרָע

A SUFFIX

Complete the Hebrew sentence:

יִהְיוּ לְרָצוֹן אִמְרֵי־ _____ וְהֶגְיוֹן _____ לְפָנֶיךָ,

יְיָ _____ _____ .

"May the words of my mouth and the thoughts of my heart be

acceptable to You, Lord, my Rock and my Redeemer".

יִ is a suffix. יִ means "my".

Four words in the sentence have the suffix יִ .

Read each Hebrew word you added to the sentence.

Do you remember the Hebrew word for "my soul"? _____

GOD'S NAME

יְיָ יְהֹוָה אֲדֹנָי אֵל אֱלֹהִים אֱלֹהַי שְׁכִינָה

God's name אֵל has different forms.

Write the two forms of אֵל found in the list above:

_____ _____

אֱלֹהַי is another way to say God's name.

Write the name here. _____

Find and lightly circle אֱלֹהַי in line 1 of the passage.

אֱלֹהַי, נְצוֹר לְשׁוֹנִי מֵרָע

Can you read lines 9 and 10 without a mistake?

Can you read lines 1-10 easily?

======= VOCABULARY REVIEW =======

Read lines 11 and 12.

The word for "peace" is _____

The word for "Israel" is _____

The two words built on the root ע‑שׂ‑ה are

_____ _____ .

Add the vowels to read the phrases:

עושה שלום במרומיו הוא יעשה שלום

The passage ends with the words וְאִמְרוּ אָמֵן.

וְאִמְרוּ אָמֵן means "and say Amen".

Do you remember the meaning of the word "Amen"?

======= READING CHALLENGE =======

Can you read the entire passage without any mistakes?

אֱלֹהַי, נְצוֹר לְשׁוֹנִי מֵרָע

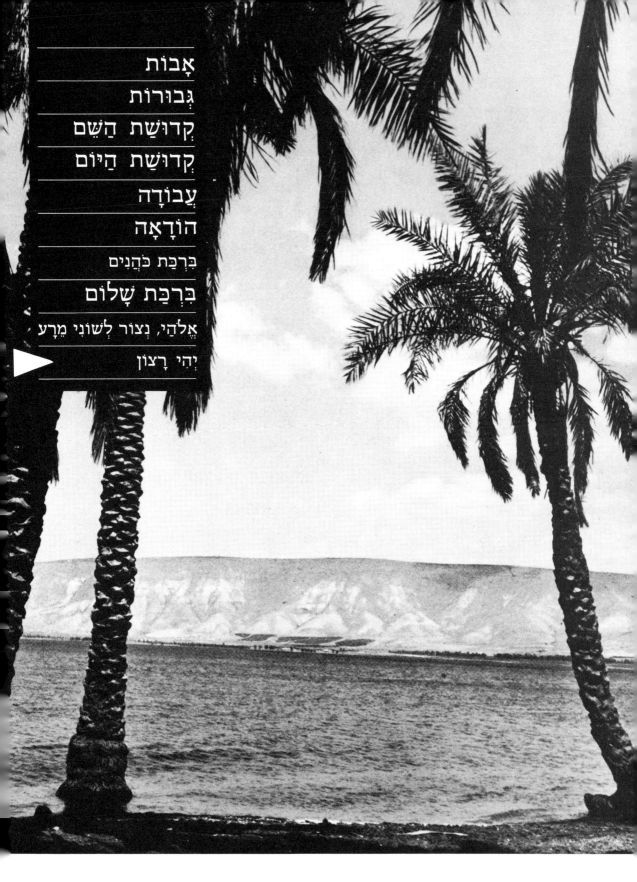

This final brief petition after the עֲמִידָה asks God to rebuild the Temple where again He will be worshiped, and to grant our portion in His Torah. This last thought completes this portion of the Shabbat Morning Service and prepares us for the Torah Service which will follow.

יְהִי רָצוֹן

1 יְהִי רָצוֹן מִלְּפָנֶיךָ, יְיָ אֱלֹהֵינוּ וֵאלֹהֵי אֲבוֹתֵינוּ,
2 שֶׁיִּבָּנֶה בֵּית הַמִּקְדָּשׁ בִּמְהֵרָה בְיָמֵינוּ, וְתֵן
3 חֶלְקֵנוּ בְּתוֹרָתֶךָ, וְשָׁם נַעֲבָדְךָ בְּיִרְאָה כִּימֵי
4 עוֹלָם וּכְשָׁנִים קַדְמֹנִיּוֹת. וְעָרְבָה לַייָ מִנְחַת
5 יְהוּדָה וִירוּשָׁלָיִם, כִּימֵי עוֹלָם וּכְשָׁנִים
6 קַדְמֹנִיּוֹת.

Write the words missing from the first line in the passage:

יְהִי רָצוֹן מִלְּפָנֶיךָ _____

The familiar phrase "our God and God of our fathers"

appears in this line.

Find the Hebrew phrase and write it here:

_____

The term for "Temple" in the passage is בֵּית הַמִּקְדָּשׁ.

Find and lightly underline the phrase in the passage.

Write the phrase here: _____

Do you recognize the root letters in הַמִּקְדָּשׁ? ___ ___ ___

What is the English meaning of the root? _____

בֵּית means "house".

How do you think the term בֵּית הַמִּקְדָּשׁ might be translated?

_____

Add the vowels to read the Hebrew:

יהי רצון מלפניך, יי אלהינו ואלהי אבותינו,
שיבנה בית המקדש במהרה בימינו

"May it be Your will, Lord our God and God of our fathers, to grant

our portion in your Torah, and may the Temple be rebuilt in our day".

═══════ **READING CHALLENGE** ═══════

Can you read lines 1 and 2 in the passage without a mistake?

═══════ **ANALYZING WORDS** ═══════

Many words in the passage end with a final letter.

Lightly circle each final letter in the passage.

Complete each column:

ם	ך	ן
_____	_____	_____
_____	_____	_____
_____	_____	
_____		

Find and lightly circle each **נוּ** ending in the passage.

Write each word here: _____ _____

_____ _____

═══════ **READING CHALLENGE** ═══════

Can you read the passage without any mistakes?

CONCLUSION

Kaddish is recited several times during the Shabbat morning service. The Kaddish looks like Hebrew but it is actually written in Aramaic. You can read Hebrew and so you can read Aramaic too! This Reader's Kaddish is recited between the עֲמִידָה and the Torah Service which follows. You will study the Kaddish, the Torah Service and selected concluding prayers in the next book.

Reader:

יִתְגַּדַּל וְיִתְקַדַּשׁ שְׁמֵהּ רַבָּא, בְּעָלְמָא דִּי בְרָא כִרְעוּתֵהּ, וְיַמְלִיךְ מַלְכוּתֵהּ בְּחַיֵּיכוֹן וּבְיוֹמֵיכוֹן וּבְחַיֵּי דְכָל-בֵּית יִשְׂרָאֵל בַּעֲגָלָא וּבִזְמַן קָרִיב, וְאִמְרוּ אָמֵן.

Congregation and Reader:

יְהֵא שְׁמֵהּ רַבָּא מְבָרַךְ לְעָלַם וּלְעָלְמֵי עָלְמַיָּא.

Reader:

יִתְבָּרַךְ וְיִשְׁתַּבַּח וְיִתְפָּאַר וְיִתְרוֹמַם וְיִתְנַשֵּׂא וְיִתְהַדָּר וְיִתְעַלֶּה וְיִתְהַלָּל שְׁמֵהּ דְּקֻדְשָׁא, בְּרִיךְ הוּא, לְעֵלָּא מִן כָּל-בִּרְכָתָא וְשִׁירָתָא תֻּשְׁבְּחָתָא וְנֶחֱמָתָא דַּאֲמִירָן בְּעָלְמָא, וְאִמְרוּ אָמֵן.

תִּתְקַבַּל צְלוֹתְהוֹן וּבָעוּתְהוֹן דְּכָל-יִשְׂרָאֵל קֳדָם אֲבוּהוֹן דִּי-בִשְׁמַיָּא, וְאִמְרוּ אָמֵן.

יְהֵא שְׁלָמָא רַבָּא מִן שְׁמַיָּא וְחַיִּים עָלֵינוּ וְעַל כָּל-יִשְׂרָאֵל, וְאִמְרוּ אָמֵן.

עֹשֶׂה שָׁלוֹם בִּמְרוֹמָיו הוּא יַעֲשֶׂה שָׁלוֹם עָלֵינוּ וְעַל כָּל-יִשְׂרָאֵל, וְאִמְרוּ אָמֵן.

יְהִי רָצוֹן